Splashes of a Brush

a colourful collection of devotional poems to inspire the soul

Laurie Konyalian

JEREMIAH HOUSE PUBLISHING

Toronto, Ontario

Copyright © 2017 Laurie Konyalian

All rights reserved. No portion of this book may be reproduced, stored in a retrieval system or transmitted in any form or by any means - electronic, mechanical, photocopy, recording, scanning, or other - except for brief quotations in critical reviews or articles, without the prior written permission of the publisher.

Published in Toronto, Ontario, Canada by Jeremiah House Publishing.

Unless otherwise noted all Scripture quotations are from the New King James Version. Copyright 1982 by Thomas Nelson, Inc. Used by permission. All rights reserved.

Scripture quotations marked (NIV) are taken from the Holy Bible, New International Version®, NIV®. Copyright © 1973, 1978, 1984, 2011 by Biblica, Inc.™ Used by permission of Zondervan. All rights reserved worldwide. www.zondervan.com The "NIV" and "New International Version" are trademarks registered in the United States Patent and Trademark Office by Biblica, Inc.™

Scriptures marked NASB are taken from the New American Standard Bible, copyright 1960, 1962, 1963, 1968, 1971, 1972, 1973, 1975, 1977 by the Lockman Foundation. Used by permission.

Konyalian, Laurie, 1981-, author
      Splashes of a brush: A colourful collection of devotional poems to inspire the soul / Laurie Konyalian.

ISBN: 978-0-9940534-6-6

Poetry / Subjects & Themes / Inspirational & Religious
Art / Subjects & Themes / Religious
Poetry / Canadian

Special Market Sales
Organizations, churches, pastors and small group leaders can receive special discounts when purchasing this book and other Jeremiah House Publishing resources. For information, please email info@jeremiahhousepublishing.com

Printed In Canada

This book of poems, songs and prayers is dedicated to the reader.

To every soul who is on a quest to encounter the Living God in a deeper way. Your Father in Heaven delights in you and is drawing you closer to Himself.

*"For He satisfies the longing soul,
And fills the hungry soul with goodness."
-Psalm 107:9*

Contents

Acknowledgements i
Endorsements iii
Preface v

1	As a Lion.	7
2	My Hand in Yours.	9
3	Astounded.	11
4	Tides.	13
5	First Place.	15
6	Inundate.	17
7	Song In The Storm.	19
8	Song at Sunrise	21
9	Awaken the Dawn	23
10	Healing Rain.	25
11	At the Sound	27
12	Bands of Love	29
13	Glory	31
14	Rest.	33
15	Imbibe.	35
16	Rising Hope.	37
17	Spontaneous Song.	39
18	Bitter into Sweet.	41
19	A Vessel.	43
20	Bloom.	45
21	The River.	47
22	Dawn	49
23	A Glimpse	51
24	Revive	53
25	Heart Song.	55
26	Seasons that Speak.	57
27	Song of the Secret Place	59
28	Christmas Song	61
29	Tidal Waves	63

Acknowledgements

Thank you Tanya Bellehumeur-Allatt for taking the time to give your endorsement of this book. You have been an encouragement to me!

A big thanks to the Toronto House of Prayer and the Quebec House of Prayer for being such a wonderful place to encounter Jesus, where heaven collides so powerfully with earth! You have played a significant part in my journey with Jesus and in the making of some of these poems and paintings.

Thank you Elsie Underwood Naraine for taking time out of your busy schedule to endorse this book and for believing in this project!

Thank you Dr. Vahe H. Apelian for being an example of one who is an excellent writer and for being an encouragement.
Thanks to all my friends who helped me realize this project by giving generously. Your kindness will never be forgotten!

Thanks mum, dad, and Sarine for encouraging me to pursue painting and writing in the first place. I don't think I would have started without that.

Thank you Jesus for making this life an exhilarating adventure, You are worth it all. This is because of You and all for Your glory!

Endorsements

In Splashes of a Brush, Laurie Konyalian has set her original poetry and artwork alongside sacred text, creating a rich visual and spiritual experience for the reader. This book is an invitation to participate in the divine conversation between the Creator and His creation through the prayerful appreciation of Konyalian's craft. Both as a devotional guide and as a source of inspiration for poets and visual artists, this book is a gift to the body of Christ.
Tanya Bellehumeur-Allatt
Founding Director, Quebec House of Prayer
Sherbrooke, Quebec, Canada

If you reach for "Splashes of A Brush" it will likely get all over you! Laurie's unique blend of poem, colour and scripture will turn your heart in the direction of your Creator! You will meet a Lion, climb a mountain, float down a river and ride the waves of the ocean! You'll watch the sun come up and go down, feel the rain falling on your thirsty soul and you'll sense the tug on your heart to kneel in reverence before the Saviour and be warmed by His love. You'll encounter your own heart of worship as you walk through the pages that lead you to Him. You will come away with honey on your lips and a light radiating the way to those who are searching for the way home!

Elsie Underwood Naraine
Lead pastor, Catch the Fire Scarborough
Scarborough, Ontario, Canada

Preface

This vivid collection of poems was written to inspire you toward a closer walk with Jesus Christ each and every day. Each poem and painting comes out of my personal encounters and walk with Him - through trial, difficulty, restful fellowship and sweet triumph!

The images and poems are based on scriptures from the Bible.

May you truly be encouraged and inspired by the pages ahead!

As A Lion

Stepping over fear,
Let us rise.

Indomitable,
Insurmountable,
Let us rise.

Bold as a lion,
Let us rise.

"Have I not commanded you?
Be strong and courageous.
Do not be afraid; do not be discouraged,
for the LORD your God will be with you wherever you go."
-Joshua 1:9 (NIV)

*"The path of the righteous
is like the morning sun,
shining ever brighter
till the full light of day."*

Proverbs 4:18 (NIV)

My Hand in Yours

I will place my hand in Yours,
As You lead me down the road,
Adventures yet untold,
Extraordinary,
And unexplored.

I will place my hand in Yours,
As the path twists and turns,
Your Word will light the way,
For each and every day.

I will place my hand in Yours,
And follow wherever You go,
Each step to unfold Your story,
To tell of Your unfading glory.

*"Behold, I stand at the door and knock.
If anyone hears My voice and opens the door,
I will come in to him and dine with him,
and he with Me."*

Revelation 3:20 (NKJV)

Astounded

*Who is He who carves the grandeur
of lofty mountain tops,
And marks off the heavens with His hand?
Yet is mindful of the sons of men?*

*Who is He who scatters stars
in their dazzling array,
And spills rays of light to awaken the dawn,
Who knows our frame,
And all of our days,
Even before one of them came to be?*

*Who is He who sets the galaxies in rotation,
And spoke the world into motion,
Who knows our every need
even before we ask of Him?*

*This is the everlasting One,
Who lives outside of time,
Yet chose to step into time,
To express the depths of His love for us.*

*This is God infinite,
Yet God intimate,
Who stoops down from the heavens,
Longing to commune with us.*

*This is the King of all kindness,
Who created us to know Him,
Who calls us to His banqueting table,
And beckons us to dine.*

Splashes of a Brush

Tides

Mercy
Flows,
Streams,
Sweeps,
Upon my soul,
Lavishly leaps.

Mercy
Swells,
Spills,
Glides,
Comes to us,
Like ocean tides.

"The steadfast love of the Lord never ceases
his mercies never come to an end;
they are new every morning;"
~Lamentations 3:22-23 (ESV)

*"You have forsaken the love you had at first [...]
Repent and do the things you did at first."*

Revelation 2:4-5 (NIV)

First Place

In the busy,
He is jealous for our gaze,
To have first place,
In the deepest part,
In the garden of our hearts.

He is beckoning us,
Close to His side,
To do the things
We did at first,
When nothing mattered more
Than just to sit at His feet.

16 | *Splashes of a Brush*

Inundate

Like bubbles
That effervesce,
Rising with
Exuberance,
Fill us,
Until we're bursting,
With heaven's joy.

"In Your Presence is fullness of joy."
Psalm 16:11 (NKJV)

*"I have set the Lord always before me;
Because He is at my right hand
I shall not be moved."*

Psalm 16:8

Song in the Storm

*Avert my gaze
From turbid waves,
To Your lovely face.*

Jesus lock my eyes on yours.

A Song at Sunrise

God my refuge,
God my friend,
Jesus Emmanuel,
With me to the end.

God my strength,
God my shield,
Father in heaven,
To You I yield.

God my Rock,
God my Lord,
Dazzling in glory,
My great reward!

God my source,
God my treasure,
Father of lights,
You love without measure!

"After these things the word of the Lord
came to Abram in a vision, saying,
"Do not be afraid, Abram. I am your shield,
your exceedingly great reward."
Genesis 15:1 (NKJV)

"My heart is fixed, O God, my heart is fixed:
I will sing and give praise.
Awaken, my glory!
Awake, lute and harp!
I will awaken the dawn."

Psalm 57:7-8 (NKJV)

Awaken the Dawn

I will come into Your courts and sing,
A song of praise,
My heartfelt offering.

I will run into Your courts and sing,
A song of thanks,
For all You've done for me.

And with my song, I will awaken the dawn,
And with this song, I will awaken the dawn!

I will set my heart on praising You,
I will set my heart on loving You.

24 | *Splashes of a Brush*

Healing Rain

*Healing rain
From heaven
Falls,
Drizzles gently
On orphaned souls.*

*Healing rain
From heaven
Falls,
Trickles timely
On heavy hearts.*

*Healing rain
From heaven
Falls,
Dancing freely
On barren lands.*

He says to us gently:
"I am the LORD who heals you."
Exodus 15:26(b) (NKJV)

"Because he has set his love upon Me,
therefore I will deliver him;
I will set him on high,
because he has known My name.
He shall call upon Me, and I will answer him;
I will be with him in trouble;
I will deliver him and honor him.
With long life I will satisfy him,
And show him My salvation."

-

Psalm 91:14-16 (NKJV)

At the Sound

*I will set my love
Upon You, my God
Even in hard seasons,
You will be the reason,
For the song of my soul.*

*I will set my love
Upon You, my Friend
You're the King most worthy,
My heart bows wholly,
At the sound of Your Name.*

28 | *Splashes of a Brush*

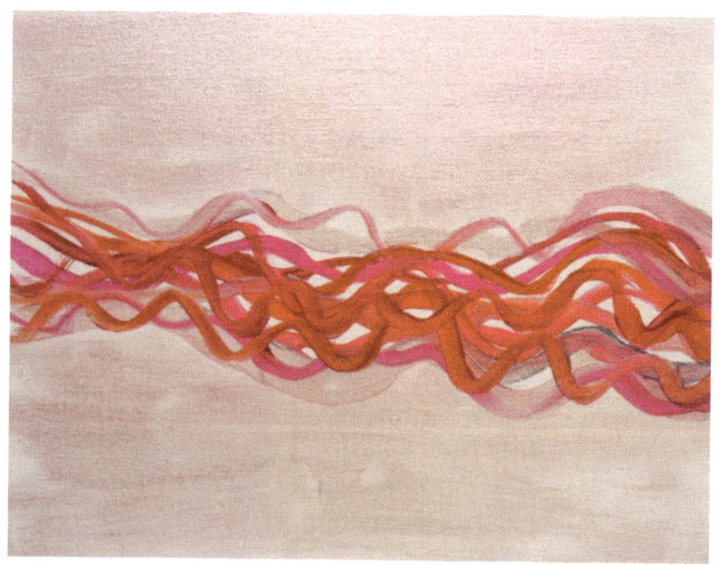

Bands of Love

*He sprinkles the stars in the heavens,
Paints sunsets of blazing glory,
And He draws us to His presence
With bands of love!*

"I drew them with gentle cords
With bands of love,"
Hosea 11:4(a) (NKJV)

Splashes of a Brush

<u>Glory</u>

Of all of that could
Wash,
Grip,
Or weigh,
Upon my very soul,
Let no other weight press upon my heart,
Like the weight of Your glory.

"Now show me your glory."
Exodus 33:18

Rest

Let me sit in Your shade,
Rest in Your Presence,
For there I find delight.

Let me sit at Your feet,
And listen to You speak,
For You have the words of life,
You alone have the words of eternal life.

"Simon Peter answered him,
"Lord, to whom shall we go?
You have the words of eternal life."
John 6:68 (NIV)

*".. that you, being rooted and grounded in love,
may be able to comprehend with all the saints
what is the width and length
and depth and height –
to know the love of Christ
which passes knowledge;
that you may be filled
with all the fullness of God."*

Ephesians 3:17-19

Imbibe

Cause me to fathom deep inside,
Widen the crevices of my soul
To imbibe,
Just how long,
How deep,
How wide,
Is Your Love,
That flows like a tide.

Let it fill the chambers of my heart,
Not just once,
But incessantly without a halt,
That I may be filled,
With the all the fullness of God!

Rising Hope

*When the storms of life foam and rage like
troubled ocean waters,
And your courage begins to wane like the
fading evening sun,
Hope in the One who is a Refuge in distress,
A Shelter from the storm.*

*His eyes of grace are on you,
And He will come to you.
There is no tempest He cannot tame,
No storm He cannot still!*

"He made the storm be still,
And the waves of the sea were hushed."
Psalm 107:29 (ESV)

38 | *Splashes of a Brush*

Spontaneous Song

Words fall short to define,
This Love that is mine,
So extravagant and free,
But I have come to clearly see,
That You came just to lavish it on me!

"See what great love the Father has lavished on us,
that we should be called children of God."
1 John 3:1 (NIV)

40 | *Splashes of a Brush*

Bitter Into Sweet

***I will remove the bitter taste that difficult circumstance has left in your mouth. My Name will be like honey on your lips, sweet to your taste.
-God***

"How sweet are your words to my taste,
sweeter than honey to my mouth!"
Psalm 119:103 (NKJV)

*"Remove the dross from the silver,
and a silversmith can produce a vessel;"*

-Proverbs 25:4 (NIV)

A Vessel

The fire in Your eyes,
Lovingly melts,
Refines,
Purges,
And Purifies.

The heat of Your gaze,
Eliminates,
Dissolves,
The dross that layers,
And dulls.

As a silversmith
Hones his work,
Here I am for You to
Fashion and forge,
Chisel and mold,
'Til I am a vessel of honor,
Of the purest gold.

<u>Bloom</u>

My heart is to see you bloom,
To see you grow,
Even in arid lands.

I delight to see your buds as they appear,
And take joy to see your petals dance in the wind.
I knew all their colors,
Even before one of them came to be.

In the very place where it was said that nothing can grow,
I speak and say that you will rise,
You will flourish.
– God

"For I know the plans I have for you,"
declares the LORD,
"plans to prosper you and not to harm you,
plans to give you hope and a future.
Jeremiah 29:11 (NIV)

46 | *Splashes of a Brush*

The River

Take me to the depths of Your River,
Where Your fullness abounds,
Where the weight of Your Presence
Invades, engulfs,
Surrounds.

Take me into the depths of Your River,
No longer to stand on its banks,
Immerse me in the pure fount of Heaven,
God my solace, my true joy giver.

Take me into the depths of Your River,
To deep waves of grace,
How I yearn to meet with You,
Heart to heart,
And face to face.

"There is a river whose streams shall make glad
the city of God,
The holy place of the tabernacle of the Most High.
God is in the midst of her, she shall not be moved;
God shall help her, just at the break of dawn."
Psalm 46:4-5 (NKJV)

*"Your love, LORD, reached to the heavens,
your faithfulness to the skies."*

Psalm 36:5 (NIV)

Dawn

Your love comforts,
Like rays of light that spill,
At the wake of dawn.

A Glimpse

I give you,
Fields of flowers,
Clouds that crown
Azure skies,
The stars that light up
The deep of night,
As a glimpse of My glory.

This temporal beauty
In all its brilliance,
Is My way of drawing you,
So we can commune.
Is My way of reminding you,
That this journey you are on
Is all about you and Me. – God

"The heavens declare the glory of God;
the skies proclaim the work of his hands.
Day after day they pour forth speech;
night after night they display knowledge."
Psalm 19:1-2 (NIV)

*"Pleasing is the fragrance of your perfumes;
your name is like perfume poured out."
No wonder everyone loves to say your name."*

Song of Solomon 1:3 (NIV & MSG)

Revive

Come like fragrance,

Come like the rain,

Jesus, come like a rush of wind,

Come like a flame!

Yes, come like a flame!

> "Set me [Jesus] as a seal upon your heart,
> as a seal upon your arm,
> for love is strong as death,
> jealousy is fierce as the grave.
> Its flashes are flashes of fire,
> the very flame of the Lord."
>
> *Song of Solomon 8:6 (ESV)*

Heart Song

I turn my gaze to Your holy face,
And worship You.

All else fades,
At Your throne of grace,
I worship You,
Yes, I will worship You!

I turn my gaze to Your holy face,
And worship You,
Yes, I will worship You!

Consume my heart,
And let it forever burn,
With this flame of first love!

56 | *Splashes of a Brush*

Seasons that Speak

As I stop to absorb the view,
I am fascinated with every hue,
That stains the leaves,
Of countless autumn trees.

The brilliance of red, orange and gold,
Transient tones,
That are hard to hold.
Although they soon fade away,
As a watch of the night,
Or the first blush of day.
They speak of one thing that will remain,
The hues of Your love,
That do not wane.

"How priceless is your unfailing love, O God!
People take refuge in the shadow of your wings."
Psalm 36:7 (NIV)

*"Yes, everything else is worthless when compared
with the infinite value of knowing
Christ Jesus my Lord."
Philippians 3:8 (NLT)*

Song of the Secret Place

Nearer to Your heart, O God,
Nearer, My Lord to You,
This is my prime pursuit,
And my sole plea.

Nearer to Your heart, O God,
Nearer, O Lord to You,
This is the longing of my soul,
My aim,
My greatest goal.

A closer walk with You, O Lord,
A closer with You,
At the cross,
I count all as loss,
Compared to the surpassing worth
Of knowing You.

A closer walk with You, O Lord,
A closer walk with You,
Looking on Your lovely face,
I press on,
To finish this race,
That began when I first said yes to You.

60 | *Splashes of a Brush*

Christmas Song

Majesty that came in meekness,
To demonstrate what true love is,
A merciful King,
Full of kindness,
A Saviour for all.

My heart with melody resonates,
As I purpose in my heart to celebrate,
The birth of Jesus my Saviour,
God incarnate,
He is for all mankind!

62 | *Splashes of a Brush*

Tidal Waves

We are loved,
Like tidal waves,
That crash over a shoreline.
Boundless,
Unstoppable,
Unrestrained.
We are loved,
Yes, we are loved by God.

To book Laurie for speaking engagements
or to order more copies of her book
"Splashes of a Brush",
Laurie Konyalian can be reached at the
following email address:

lauriekonyalian@gmail.com

Other Titles From Jeremiah House Publishing Available on Amazon.com

Lily Among Thorns - Mia Christine
lily among thorns gives creative guidance to finding contentment in a world of never enough. For every heart overwhelmed with disappointment, difficulty and the uncertainty of life, these poems, songs, and short stories trumpet bold statements for resilient living, leading the unsatisfied into lasting joy and freedom.

Awaken My Heart: *Listening For The Still Small Voice* - Julia McDonald
Follow Julia on her journey through the Psalms and Proverbs, as she shares lessons from her personal devotionals and then, begin your own! Fill the pages with your own prayers and insights as you search for God in the scriptures. Today is the day for your heart to be awakened to a more intimate relationship with God!

Money Mindset SHIFT. Church Edition: *The Top 9 Myths that Keep Christians Stuck Financially And How To Get Unstuck, Live Debt Free and Build Wealth!* - Toyin Crandell
High performance mindset and finance coach Toyin Crandell helps Christians called to the marketplace identify the top 9 myths specific to Christians that keep you stuck financially and how to get unstuck, live debt free and build a legacy of wealth for generations - to the glory of God.

Making Your Marriage Work, Maama's Practical Wisdom For A Lasting, Happy Marriage - Eyitayo Dada
Marriage is not meant to be endured, it is meant to be enjoyed. Too many couples are either bored or holding on "for God's sake" or "for the sake of their children". With practical advice based in the word of God, this book will help revive the joy, passion and laughter in your marriage.